Photographs by Tom Stoddart and Alastair Thain

Edge of Madness

Sarajevo, a city and its people under siege

Royal Festival Hall

Edge of Madness is a study by two British photographers
of the siege of Sarajevo, the longest in modern European
history. For Tom Stoddart the exhibition represents a fitting
conclusion to the four years he spent documenting the lives
of the besieged citizens of the city. For Alastair Thain it
represents an opportunity to apply his vision and his unique
camera designs to a complex and emotive subject. But above
all, it is the aim of both photographers that the exhibition stands
as a tribute to the courage and dignity shown by ordinary
people caught in the crossfire of war.

Many deserve special recognition for their contribution to this
project, and none more than our principal sponsor, Camelot
Group plc. Without their generous support, this exhibition and
catalogue would not have been possible.

Special thanks must also go to Metro Imaging, who printed
Tom Stoddart's work and provided substantial darkroom space
for Alastair Thain to make his enormous prints. Many thanks
to Daniel Glasser for his diligence and skill in printing Tom's
pictures and to Adrian Tilley for his calmness and clarity of
thought in supervising both print jobs.

For additional support and help in-kind we are grateful to
Trudie Styler, The Sunday Times Magazine, Philip Morris,
Agfa Gevaert AG and Ilford Imaging Ltd.

Last, our sincere thanks go to Martin Bell for contributing
such an insightful essay to this catalogue and for his
appreciation of the photojournalist's profession.

John Easterby
Editor
Independent Photographers Group

Joanne Bernstein
Visual Arts Programmer
Royal Festival Hall, SBC

*All proceeds from the sales of this catalogue will be donated to
Children's Aid Direct in support of their humanitarian activities
around the world.*

*In their brief history, Children's Aid Direct have reached more
than 1 million children and their carers and are actively
engaged in support projects on all sides of the political divide
in Bosnia.*

*In the last 16 years the number of children affected by war has
quadrupled from 6 million to 24 million. The figure is predicted
to escalate to 31 million by the year 2000.*

"Shoot at slow intervals until
I order you to stop. Shell them until
they can't sleep, don't stop until
they are on the edge of madness"
Ratko Mladić

Introduction by Martin Bell

The war recedes from news and passes into history, to be replaced by the most primitive form of peace, which is no more than an absence of fighting. Since I left Bosnia in April 1996, resolving not to return, I have discovered that it is easier to take the reporter out of the war zone than the war zone out of the reporter. No, I don't think I am obsessed by it, but it gave me plenty to think about – which is why I subtitled my book on it the 'Reflections of a War Zone Thug'.

Trying to distil some coherence from these experiences, which mattered to me more than anything else that I have lived through, I have come to sum them up in a series of 'H' words. One of these is Horror. I had not expected to witness such things done by neighbour to neighbour in supposedly civilised Europe. Another is Hatred, I had not expected to see such hatred either. But a third 'H' word is of a different order, and that is Heroism. People sometimes ask me what it is that drives a journalist to be a war reporter – or, having become one, to remain one (and believe me, there are many who think better of it). Leaving aside the fact that it tends to happen by accident, the easy answer is that it offers a ringside seat at the making of history and events of great consequence: there may be trivial election campaigns, but there are few trivial wars. But a deeper reason is that war reporters, in simply going about their business, will find themselves privileged to keep the company of heroes – not exclusively or even principally heroes in uniform, but ordinary people who stand against the savagery of the times and risk their lives to save lives. Wars bring out the best as well as the worst in people. All three of the communities of Bosnia had an abundance of such heroes. So did the aid agencies, and the regiments from many armies who served under the UN's blue helmets. Even that lowly and despised under-class, the foreign journalists, were moved from time to time by the suffering of the innocent to step outside their traditional role as suppliers of snap-shots and sound bites. I do not believe that we were very effective, but we tried to help where we could.

There is one more defining 'H' word – a word now out of fashion and not much used. It may be due for a revival. That word is Honour. To help people whom we have it in our power to help – I can see honour in that. To try to help such people and for one reason or another to miscalculate and fail – I can see honour also in that. But in not trying to help them at all I see no honour. And in walking away from those whom we are mandated to help, and authorised to protect under a resolution of the United Nations Security Council (it was called the UN Protection Force, wasn't it?), and to leave them to be massacred in a UN-protected 'Safe Area' – there is surely dishonour in that. And in the decisions not taken, the help not given, the symbolic actions disguising inaction – there is dishonour in those as well.

At least the United Nations, following its retreats and defeats in both Bosnia and Somalia, is under new management and studying what went wrong. It actually has a 'Lessons Learned Unit' in its Department of Peacekeeping Operations in New York. Maybe the rest of us should do the same, for we all have lessons to learn – politicians, aid workers, soldiers and even journalists. The record of the journalists, who are too much given to self-praise (for if we don't praise ourselves, who will do it for us?), is hardly one of flawless professional performance. I myself made many mistakes in Bosnia, mostly from the habit of travelling around the landscape under the armoured protection of the helpful British Army. It wasn't the soldiers' fault: it was mine. Looking back on it now, I believe that all those Warriors and Scimitars and the rest of the military rolling stock kicked up so much dust in my eyes that it blinded me to events of great and grim consequence taking place elsewhere in the country. We neither reached them nor reported them; and when rumours of them filtered out much later they made me deeply aware, and ashamed, of the risks that I had not taken.

Let us then by all means establish our 'Lessons Learned Unit' – even if it be only in the mind, as a process of inquiry and reflection; for there is no point surviving these experiences if we do not learn from them, and if we fail to acknowledge our mistakes we are probably doomed to repeat them. A permanent record would be useful for such an enterprise. We need something more than our frail memories to remind us what this war was and how it developed, and what the outside world did that it shouldn't have done, and shouldn't have done that it did. The record could serve as a kind of monument and a standing reproach to us all.

As a TV reporter, which is what I am, I might be expected to argue for the primacy of moving images as the principal medium of record. The Bosnian war was a television war. Though some of its battles were fought out of the sight of television, much of it – including most notably the siege of Sarajevo – occurred under the camera's eye. Vivid images of minor skirmishes were flashed around the world in living colour and with blazing sound-tracks; the major bombardments of the capital were beamed into the living rooms of the world on the same day that they happened. It was like a three and a half year mini-series: a war not fought for television – it would have started as it did whether our transmission systems had been satellites or cleft sticks – but fought on television. And it happened at a point of intersection between television and warfare, when the means of mass destruction – like a 500 pound aircraft bomb rocket-propelled onto a city centre – coincided with the means of mass communication, that the resulting carnage would reach a world-wide audience within minutes of the event. This is changing the practice of warfare, and of diplomacy.

And yet the televised images of war, so wrenching and full of impact at the time, are less effective as a permanent record, a living and lasting archive. This is in the nature of the medium: my medium, so I know its shortcomings. It is transitory and ephemeral. It moves and passes and vanishes into the ether. Its images are stored on tape and not instantly accessible. A man cannot set himself down before one of them and study it for as long as he likes. It may be our primary source of news or at least of impressions about the news; but on a longer view it is rather hard to learn from. Photographs are different. Even in black and white – perhaps especially in black and white – they have the nowness and thereness of the single frozen moment. The art of the photographer is to find and freeze the moment.

But it is a dangerous occupation. It is on any rational consideration a truly daft way to earn a living – yes, even dafter than mine. It is lonely, unpensionable and notoriously underpaid. The combat photographer takes greater risks than his opposite number in television. He cannot stand off at a distance and rely on a long lens and a sound-track to see him through. He works in close-up. That means being close to too many snipers and crawling around in too many fields of fire.

So it was that in the wars of ex-Yugoslavia, which claimed the lives of more than 50 journalists, the highest casualties as a group were taken by the still photographers. Yet these were also the people given the least protection by those who employed them and who profited from their courage.

Tom Stoddart

Some were freelances without commissions, and with no one to turn to in an extreme emergency. From the start to finish of the war, most of them went without the logistic support that we in the BBC regarded as standard issue: an armoured vehicle, a supply line, a training in fieldcraft and battlefield first aid. Some of them lacked even body armour. They were living, it seemed to us, on the edge of madness. *Edge of Madness*: what more suitable title for an exhibition of photographs from the Bosnian war? Of the two lens artists represented here, Alastair Thain is the one who came to it after the event, bringing with him a camera which he developed from NASA's space age technology and which surpassed the powers of the human eye itself. The warscapes of Sarajevo, in all their sweep and detail, are his work.

Tom Stoddart, the other photographer, is a pioneer of a different sort: of combat camerawork and the art of survival in the world's most dangerous war zone. Almost inevitably he became one of its casualties. Running under fire and diving for cover outside the Parliament Building, he broke his ankle in six places and his shoulder. (Let it be noted that The Sunday Times, for whom he was working, stood by him and met its obligations honourably; not all wounded snappers were so fortunate.) Tom returned to Bosnia a year later. He had unfinished business there. He went on to prove that a dodgy ankle and a titanium shoulder are no impediment to the practice of world-class photography.

Alastair Thain

Now the business is finished. This exhibition, which draws a line under it, is by no means a sample cross-section of his work. The scenes of combat and bloodshed have been deliberately omitted, to provide a sharper focus on what remains: a portrait of people in warfare. Very few of them are armed or in uniform. They are victims, survivors and heroes. This is in line with recent trends in war reporting, which focuses less on the strategies and weapons systems used in a war and more on the people caught up in it. We have been trying to humanise our business.

There can be no nostalgia for those tragic times in Sarajevo, which for more than three years was the world's most notorious shooting gallery. Tom Stoddart's images are a reminder of this, and of the terror and grief that went with it. But they also catch and communicate the dignity of people: people whose only task was survival and who would not let the war defeat them. (I believe this to have been true on both sides of the front lines.)

I remember Haris Silajdzic, who was Bosnia's Prime Minister at the time, returning from a visit to one of the Gulf states appalled by the money-driven nature of its society: a people facing West not to Mecca but only to their own oilfields. He was relieved to return to his embattled Sarajevo, where there was no economy and nothing was being produced but explosions – but where there was dignity and civility, where people helped each other, and every day's survival was another small victory.

Edge of Madness is a memorial to those times. It demands attention and rewards reflection. Its message is simple and serious.

Lest we forget.

The main arterial road in Sarajevo became known as 'Snipers Alley' where hundreds of lives were lost during the four year siege. Each day as people moved around the city trying to find food, fuel or water, they fell under the deadly telescopic sights of the surrounding Bosnian Serb forces. Commuting to work Sarajevo-style required flat shoes, fitness and the courage to run across the most dangerous intersections in the world.

Sarajevo's graveyards bear testament to the bloody siege which lasted more than 1,000 days and killed 12,000 of its citizens.

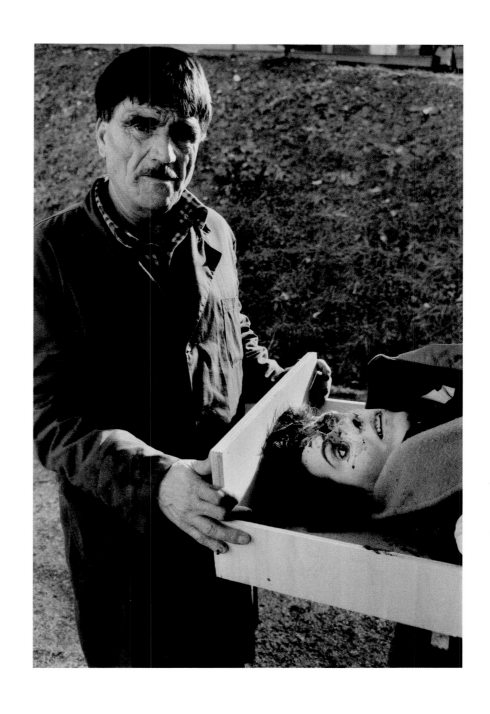

Looking proud and dignified, Meliha Vareshanovic makes her way through Dobrinja, one of Sarajevo's most dangerous suburbs. Her message to the surrounding Serbs is simple: *you will never defeat us!*

Bullets and shells were no respecters of innocence during the dark days of the siege. Children died, or were wounded while playing outside in the dangerous streets and open spaces. Thousands of others became malnourished from existing on a diet of humanitarian aid.

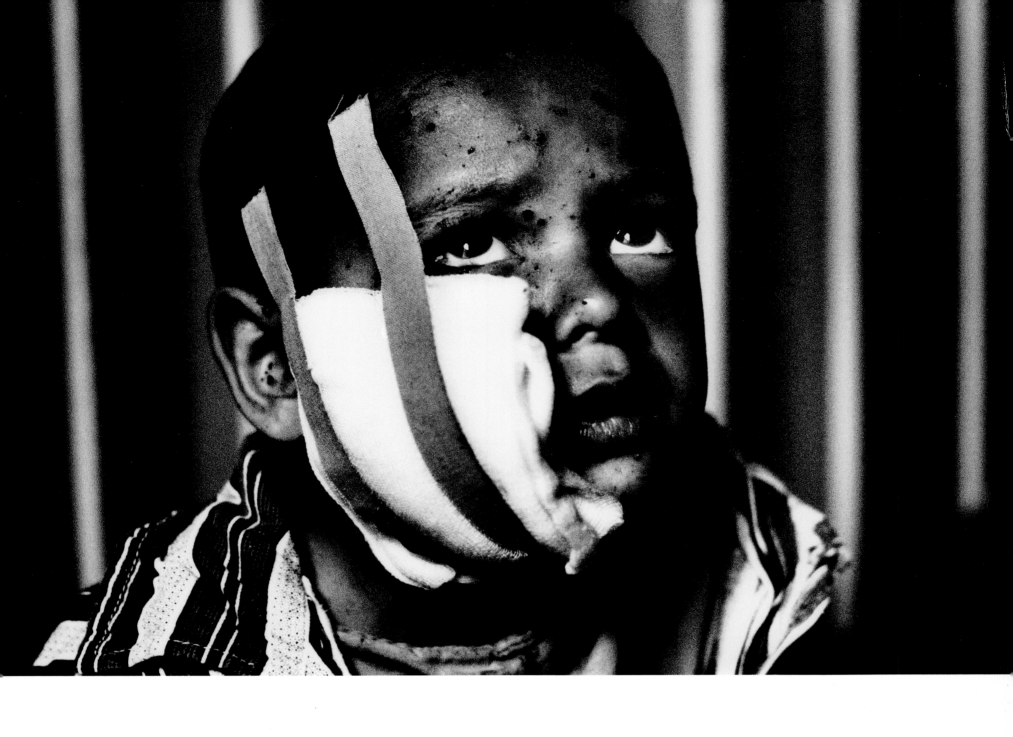

Sarajevo's broken streets and homes will be rebuilt quickly, but it will take generations before the broken lives of its people recover from the war.

Acknowledgements

So many people lent their support and help to this project, both in Sarajevo and in the UK, that it would be impossible to name them all. To all those people, no matter how great or small their contribution, Tom Stoddart and Alastair Thain extend their gratitude.

In particular, Tom Stoddart would like to thank his translator Aida Cavdar for her friendship and bravery and her family for their shelter during his time in Sarajevo. To Aidan Sullivan of the Sunday Times Magazine, together with his editors who fulfilled their responsibilities to a photojournalist injured in the field and to Mr. Fergus Patterson of the Cromwell Hospital for his surgical skill. Many thanks to Geoff Katz, Steve Blogg and all the staff at Katz pictures for their unflinching support.

Tom gives special thanks to Kate Hoey for her personal support. He thanks his friends and family and would like to use this occasion to remember his parents Tommy and Kathleen and Larry Bartlett whose absence is sadly missed.

Alastair Thain gives special thanks to his partner Tracey, his mother Lois and family, Jackie, Rory, Tiffany, Janet, India and Dylan. Many thanks to Jeff Lawrence and Harry Baker at Ronford-Baker Engineering. Thanks also go to Ron Hodge. In particular Alastair thanks Aletheia Gentle for her friendship and support. His final thoughts are in loving memory to his father.

The photographers would jointly like to thank John Easterby, Androna Calles and Lisa Pritchard of the Independent Photographers Group for their affection and dedication, Quentin Newark and David Hawkins of Atelier for designing the catalogue and exhibition so beautifully, the British Army for their logistical support, Joanne Bernstein and all the team at the Royal Festival Hall and catalogue printers Jevons Brown.